THE WOMB AND THE MIND

Duane Vorhees

ISBN: 978-81-19228-38-6

First Edition: 2023
Rs. 200/-

Cyberwit.net
HIG 45 Kaushambi Kunj, Kalindipuram
Allahabad - 211011 (U.P.) India
http://www.cyberwit.net
Tel: +(91) 9415091004
E-mail: info@cyberwit.net

Contents

WE ARE THE PROGENY OF THE BIG BANG 7
OUR PLACE IN SPACE 8
AMERICSSON 9
O NIGHT, THE DOMAIN OF OUR DREAMS 10
THE SINS OF POETS AND PASTORS 11
TELL ME. ARE YOU SURE? 12
QUANDARY 13
THE PROCESS 14
REPAST, RESTORE, REPOSE 15
BARTER 16
A REALIZATION OF LENT 17
OFFERINGS TO THE LORD 18
VERTEBRATE EVOLUTION 19
A QUESTION OF BEAUTY 20
PANTHEON 21
FARMERSVILLE TO HERE 22
AT YOUR GATE 23
ADAM AND EVE AND ENTROPY 24
COMMUNION 26
CURTAINS 27
WHY WE CANCELED THE RAPTURE 28
GOING OUT IN STYLE 29
SUNSHINE PACT 30
SOME FOUR OR FIVE DESCENTS SINCE 31
THAT ANCIENT GENTRIFICATION 32
AMPHIBIANS 33
CORRECT ATTRIBUTION 34
THE WOMB AND THE MIND 35
TO BUILD A POEM 36

MELETUS 37
ENGINE 38
RISERS 39
ELMER TERMAGANTRY PARADISE BROCHURE 40
LONGEVITY AND POPULAR SUCCESS 41
MYTHTORY 42
ANTHRACNOSE AND ADULTHOOD 43
AFTER THAT EDGE 44
DANCE 45
GRAY AND PRIVATE 46
MANWISE-WISE 47
METEOROLOGY 48
ALAS, ALONE 49
INDIVIDUAL, OF A GROUP 50
THERE IS NO IS NO WILL BE 52
THE DIFFERENCE BETWEEN 53
WHY POETRY FAILED 54
CHOICES 55
BEFORE YOU ANSWER 56
LEGACY 57
WHICH CHANGES CHANGE AGAIN 58
THE SOON, THE THEN, AND THE NOW 59
WORLDS LIVE ON BEYOND OUR WALLS
AND CURTAINS 60
PROFESSIONS 61
NO APOLOGY, APOLLO 62
O, DEMOCRACY 63
WHAT MAY BE AND WHAT WILL 64
THE COROLLARY 65
WITNESSING 66
AND WE'VE NO ARTHUR 67
AN ESSAY CONCERNING HUMAN UNDERSTANDING 68
CONFESSIONS 69

DOWSER 71
PROPERTIES 72
REFLECTIONS ON ERASMUS QUELLINUS II, CUPID ON A DOLPHIN, MUSEO DEL PRADO, MADRID 73
MARILYN 74
DEAR READER 75

WE ARE THE PROGENY OF THE BIG BANG

I'm no comet, no constellation,
just a telescope on our sky,
observatory of meteors
and moonly progress.

I see we are not ourselves only
but also parallels and echoes
of the ones who came before.

Not only our own singularities,
but also we are in part products
of our planet's climes, times,
crimes. Properties of
the universal particles.

The passed is my present,
given for your predictions,
as light is the shadow
of infinity's origin.

OUR PLACE IN SPACE

Our egg and our girdle – from our toelines to stars' beyonds,
edgeless sky occupies. Continents and constellations
indicate sky's compass points in all directions.
Here, and there, it corrals our air. Sky's only brake is our imagination:
We house our deities in this infinite bubble, map every manifestation
of this cosmic envelope. We extract our character and extort destinies
through constant observation, keen ingenuity, endless speculation
as we contemplate wonderingly at sky's progress and creation.

AMERICSSON

Whores parade their hymens
and diplomats their swords.
Priests display their diamonds.

With confusion since birth
futures ignore their pasts.

Cowards hang their medals
and gluttons wear their fasts.

The sugar tastes bitter
from the sweat of the slaves.

All the stones and banners
can't cover all the graves.

The lame think they're dancers.
The blind behave like seers.
The deaf play musician.

Hiding behind paved mirrors,
the meek show ambition.

Our clear insight is blurred.

O NIGHT, THE DOMAIN OF OUR DREAMS

The full world by day
is a speckled shade,
but colors at night
all coordinate.

Our humanity
claims its sanity's
enshrined in marble
but held together
by spirit and breath,
yet we live in dust
and we choose to starve
amidst much rich stock.

Only dark's tattoo
clears checkered shadows.

THE SINS OF POETS AND PASTORS

When preachers and poets exercise
our metaphorical rhetoric
we much prefer the dramatic
—the pitchfork of lightning—
above the anticlimactic
—a blanket of sunshine.
The wrinkled and crippled shall arise
sooner than the smooth and the spry.
The salve is shadowed by the sting,
and Found, by Wandering.
The tornado and the torrent
and the volcano's ring
are prized beyond plastic ornaments.
We tend to the tortured and the tried.

TELL ME. ARE YOU SURE?

I wonder if once half our limbs were wings, like a fowl,
or if they all had thumbs once. Or is that only now?
The asker wants to know.
Do we see us in mirrors, or need a fluoroscope?
Are lovers on the level or are they on a slope?
This doubter wants to know.
Was Tigris always Tigris or once was it Paradise?
Was Jesus a carpenter or always just a christ?
This skeptic wants to know.
Are the answers on the internet? Or in ourselves?
Or should I communicate with oracles and elves?
This searcher wants to know.
We learn through maturity? But ages are cages….
Or from these ancient books of fingered, faded pages?
Don't we all want to know?

QUANDARY

Flatter me – Do I receive or repeat?
With contempt or reciprocity?

THE PROCESS

My appetite
is my engine.

I transubstantiate
the wine of night
to morning wind,
body to pulsed headache state.
And I might write
undisciplined
doggerel to celebrate.

I eat that shite.
I take it in
and digest it. I translate
rails into kites
and doubt to djinn;
vomit; and hope it pulsates.

REPAST, RESTORE, REPOSE

Even after time, the past and
our endeared tradition will come
back. We'll hoard once more our futures
as we again find position.
Like the vine embraces the pine.

BARTER

I'll grasp your rose if you embrace my thorn
the gardener told the florist
I'll taste your fruit if you endure my mud
the planter said to the grocer
and the jeweler promised the farmer
to gem gardens and zircon skies,
to exchange for diamonds and jet
the world's nectar and ambrosia
and we'll share our pain and prosperity
lovers to lovers always said

A REALIZATION OF LENT

The stars sparkle in the dark,
their teeth flash like whetted saws.
Harems in Shahanshah's parks
are the whores at Mardi Gras.
From the sky they cut and bite,
promise to shred me to dust.
But with the coming of light
Shah's lust has whittled to thirst
and the blades vanished to rust.

OFFERINGS TO THE LORD

Our parents are reminders
of fertility they lost:
the forests of pine; myrhh;
the First Fruits of Pentecost;
forever tracts of bluebells;
the fields, of cotton and maize,
of asters and asphodels,
that yield crops beyond praise;
and the tree that bore the fruit
that forfeited our birthright.

My calling is to reroot
our garden, without the blight.
Yours is to be the herder
of beast names Father assigned.
Remember: we are brothers
and not each other's minders.

VERTEBRATE EVOLUTION

You, sweet guest at a sugared feast,
soon may just be dust in a seared waste.
Today I carry the lash
but tomorrow wear the leash.
Fates and fortunes shift and swerve.
Voices drift from noise to verse.
Some of us skeletons shall end as relics.

A QUESTION OF BEAUTY

Are you, my dear, a sloth,
agnostic of appearance?
Maybe your self's a ghost
and you depend on your clothes.
Your beauty, inherent
or of workmanship a boast?

PANTHEON

Whose slaves are we and the world?
Maya's
Dreams of tomorrows
children:
twirl with the Milky Way,
Vishnu,
feast on wine and bread
Jesus,
and die and die and die
Buddha,
among the stones and sand and stars.
Allah....

FARMERSVILLE TO HERE

I had friends and family,
library books, dreams, and chores.
Although I had no money
I never felt I was poor.
I observed the mystery
of virgin then wanton girls.
And the kissings and whiskey
drew me to these further shores
where new friends and family
are my silver and my pearls.
My chores became my duty
and my memories my lore.

AT YOUR GATE

Be careful! There's a charmer
who's smiling at your gate.
He may be selling dharma,
he may be selling hate.
It may be he's a Witness
or one with a hit list.
He may be selling makeup,
he may be selling plates.
Or you may be a Jacob
who's wrestling with your fate.

ADAM AND EVE AND ENTROPY

But Newton's
apple tree
took root,
bore fruit
as infinity's
axle tree.

My universe
comprises
my consciousness.
But for a part
of the heart
of time
we entwined—
your universe
and mine
embraced,
shared space.

Your-near-my-far
showed no gulf
until time—
diamond mine
studded with stars—
time — swallowed itself.
Our universe,
our consciousness,
exited existence.

But galaxies
of progeny
expanded eternity.

COMMUNION

God gave us our nakedness,
the bulge and curves
that enmuse and then infuse
the poet's words.
And so, as now we embrace
infinity,
I don't ask you to undress
virginity
but request you to address
divinity.

CURTAINS

Timeless time installs secret police
to dictate behind the curtain.
They implant gametes of disease.
They spin planets of burden
and split elements of my ease.
Rain clouds resting on the mountain's breast
shed tears of iron, tears of pearl.
My armored ecstasy goes rust.
The double helix uncurls.
My marble agony goes dust.

WHY WE CANCELED THE RAPTURE

Jesus resurrected in our holy land
where gain is encouraged to slay disabled
where children are butchered in wombs and schools

where locusts are hoisted above the lambs
where phallic politicos prize wombs not women
where angels abandoned the light on the hill

where we clutter our havens with dangers and snares
and prioritize a bloated right over our lives
where from pulpit and press we propagate lies, denigrate knowledge

where character is created by tears and tears
where donors laugh and voters die
where an amendment is worshiped to sacrifice its body

where we tup our neighbors' asses
where differences are mocked and punished, heroes condemned, wicked honored
and martyrs and prophets are corporate shills

where we give to caesars what is not the Caesar's
where we romanticize stars and bastardize the earth.
We assassinate ourselves. We unsweetened the honey, soured the milk.

So the Jesus resurrected we again crucified.
And since we do know that which we do
he didn't ask his father us to forgive.

GOING OUT IN STYLE

It may be when all carousing is done
I'll find myself back where I began,
one component in a cosmic union
or driftwood in an eternal ocean.

I have ordered up the diet of worms
from that fashionable Hall of Nothing
noted for its decor of wreaths and urns.

I've selected appropriate clothing,
so I'm confident I will look my best
before appearance is invisible.

After raucously trading shots with Death
I'll be ready for the quiet and still.

My body is a hospice, not an inn,
nowhere to enjoy but one to die in.

SUNSHINE PACT

Love did survive the midnights
though when we swore each other
our love would last forever
we meant mainly in sunlight.

But at last it was the fire
that burned us into liars.

SOME FOUR OR FIVE DESCENTS SINCE

Natural selection's neutral
in terms of progress and morals.
Random goes unpredictable—
noble or reprehensible.
Once, in effect, we had five hands—
two top, two down, and one behind.
We lost our old prehensile tails—
the cost of opposable thumbs.
We got better, sensible brains
by trading touch for cranium.

THAT ANCIENT GENTRIFICATION

Your good neighborhood is rezoned.
The lawns have given way to bones,
mausoleums of expired hours,
and dank granite-dungeoned towers.
After your last mortgage was paid
the real estate mortician made
that inevitable deal: Trade
your habit-practiced house of flesh
for a dormitory of death.

AMPHIBIANS

Part of us is feather,
another is anvil.
As reptiles of reason
and fishes of passion
we are amphibians
that define the betweens,
a muddle of middles
among brakes and throttles.
And the trajectories
of our biographies
trace patterns of lurches
and runs and reverses
and rises and lunges
and ripraps and wrenches
and pauses and passes
and misses and catches.
Ah! Those rubs and doublings.

CORRECT ATTRIBUTION

The thrust, parry, and riposte
are claimed by the saber,
yet, the point, the edge, the hilt
imply a duelist.

As though there were no poet,
the pen boasts the epic;
and the hammer, the palace
as though no architect.

So do not infer agents
are the inspiration.

THE WOMB AND THE MIND

Linen yokes do unlaw
and straw diplomas unlearn.
We struggle for crust and meat
in the midst of our famine.
And the wayfarer is ever rootless.

The judges emasculate given rights
through the abrogation of juries.
Their jailers encage physicality
to moralize our histories.

Existence is dust and heat,
and darkness in the cavern.
But the warfarer is never bootless.

When aborters eliminate life
it's a plunder of ovaries;
when censors murder immortality,
a massacre of libraries.

We lack math to square the parabola
and the grammar to parse the parables.

TO BUILD A POEM

To make a poem
with truth and scope,
easiness,
and slide

you need to join
a lute, some rope,
a Vesey desk,
and a guy.

(The guy holds it true, desk allows the huge, rope ties it in place, and lute sets the pace.)

MELETUS

The critic is Utopian
and imagines a perfect art.
The judge condemns the creator,
who inevitably falls short.
But a dream is not a vision.

The builder constructs a chapel,
inspector applies wrong blue print
and thus disallows the crapper.

The prophets develop the Way
as they perform their miracles.
The inquisitor denounces
the heresies of those martyrs.

Navigators align new sails
which assessors label ballast.

Truest poets are inventors,
critics anti-iconoclasts.

Old chestnuts remain ever green:
Introducers of novelty
will be called by academics
traducers of antiquity.

ENGINE

Nature's innovator
and great conservator.
Blind and invisible,
bats and chameleons.
The wheels of change/not change,
chains and dirigibles,
engine evolution.

RISERS

The have-nots who succeed the haves
fail to fortress against have-nots:
erasers execute pencils,
appetite outdoes position,
the valleys overtake the hills,
well-placed whispers silence trumpets,
the crippled one called Dare-To-Brave
soon outpaces Satisfaction,
Beauty seduces Intellect,
Hungry swallows Content piecemeal,
Necessity trumps Discretion,
the pauper apes the pompous ways.

ELMER TERMAGANTRY PARADISE BROCHURE

The yards and gardens yawn unkempt. They're bare
of herbs, but the weeds
prosper in Heaven

while fat jackals congregate in their lair
and consume more fleece
and flesh of brethren.

The tableau sharpens itself in the glare:
promises of grace
sold to unshriven
sinners beyond any conscience or care.

Abandoned dovecotes ceded to ravens.
Dogs and drunkards sleeping everywhere,
every one at peace
in their haven.

[Sinclair Lewis wrote about Elmer Gantry, an unholy evangelist. Medieval Christians falsely believed that Muslims worshipped a goddess named Termagant.]

LONGEVITY AND POPULAR SUCCESS

Pick your sect, any sect,
and open accompanying texts
of wondrous stories
from one page to the next
of checks and then glory,
of godliness and gore.

MYTHTORY

Kronos swallowed Jonah,
sparing Noah's bayan ark,
while Vishnu churned the sea,

and Typhon birthed Leviathan
when he halved the Sea of Reeds.

Jesus chopped down the banyan
they called Yggdrasil
and carved it into a cross.

Then he crucified Buddha and Odin
and all the other gods.

ANTHRACNOSE AND ADULTHOOD

When I was half my size
I'd ladder branch-by-branch
to share bird-and-leaf chants
with an enabling sky.

Quiet amidst the bark,
I surveyed the hard brown
boundary of the down,
saw stark marks of earthdark.

Serene and unjaded
by budgets and markets
or badges and helmets,
I floated unweighted.

Now I've doubled my height,
and sky's beyond my reach.
The blackness became bleached
and I've made peace with blight.

AFTER THAT EDGE

was was is is is was
some say Eternity
some Annihilation
a slice of a moment
tinier than a now

DANCE

We cling to our same
til events force change.
The anxious dancer
transforms. A wrestler
who can grasp and hold
and grapple and throw
responds but begins
then the dance again.
And thus a wax melts
and fills a new mold.

GRAY AND PRIVATE

Our best pastors and princes,
otherwise trusted and wise,
may pitch sensitive business
with their bastard or mistress
on whom, through love, they rely.

The celebrity achieved
by their close execution
is aided by secrecy
—it's disguised as modesty—
and humble expectations.

By gray and private players
publics may be better served
than by open purveyors
of position, rule, and prayer.
Great straight pitchers may throw curves.

MANWISE-WISE

Man has three developmental stages:
the Is, the Will Be, and the Will to Be.
This trinity of phases are cages
that invent and identify the beasts
that advance/inhibit humanity
(the frustrations, efforts, failures, rages,
aspirations, successes, tragedies...)—
Their interactions provide the pages
of plots, characters, chords, scores, melodies
that fuel our opera-biographies.

METEOROLOGY

withstand the waters and the winds and the weathers
as well as you can
and extend to neighbors and strangers
your wet and tempes'd hand
some of you will float
and some may fall
but you'll survive the world's storms
together

ALAS, ALONE

Alas, alone
we can do
just so much.

But,
together,
so much less.

INDIVIDUAL, OF A GROUP

Any cluster forms a culture.

You maintain you're a person
in full possession of your acts,
but you obey your nation,
follow in the tracks of your pack.

There is a culture for the rice field,
a culture for the street,
one for the sword and shield,
and one for defeat.

You have a class, you have a caste.

That atom you think is you
fits the periodic table,
The island you call your soul
conjoins an archipelago.

There's a culture for the broken,
a culture for the brave.
There's one for the chosen,
and one for the prey,

You have a clan, you have a band.

You honor your profession,
and you adhere to family.

You share in a confession,
and you're part of humanity.

There's a culture for the winners,
a culture for the lost.
There's one for the swimmers,
and one for the dust.

Any clutter has some cultures.

THERE IS NO IS NO WILL BE

We have no claims on inexistent
futures or less-than-a-point presents
that pass before forming a moment.
Memory and imagination
engage to impose domination,
yet we can possess only our pasts
plus our self's sense, senses, flesh, and breath.

THE DIFFERENCE BETWEEN

Chain mail is not the habit of the naked prophet, it's worn by the lanced and shielded knight. But the dungeon finds them both.

All the mail is stamped and opened, but your body's an envelope that holds intact your message til you're delivered out of mankind.

The universal yeast rises you in a puffy crust, though the oven's soon extinguished.

Stones are on a downward course, fire's on an upward, and you a leveling.

Death is the difference between the doing and the done.

You write your script for fortune and immortality, and some one attends your theater to splurge on popcorn. The curtain closes the set. Discredits roll.

The time comes to join the ranks of after-time. Army succumbs to armistice.

WHY POETRY FAILED

The poets were once the doctors and prophets of the world.

Needing ready rhymes, they mixed in their ceramic pestles
burrs with pearls.

Their cloisters
conveniently alternated figures like Zeus
and Jesus.

Their unguents and prescriptions confounded tinctures and blood.

Their sonnets had descriptions of birds, but of the vultures
or the doves?

Their sutures
and their stanzas were insufficient for the bleeding
or reading.

CHOICES

Voyages and sowing done,
toilers of the sea and soil
enjoy city noise and boil,
the choices and strange voices.
They employ its ointments and oils.

These hoi polloi avoid
the royal ploys and poisonings
that roil the hoity-toity
who toy with boycotts,
with turmoil and spoil.

BEFORE YOU ANSWER

Would you be the ant or the antelope?
Strong to stay or quick to fly?

But recall:
the stalwarts who can't cope
likely die.

LEGACY

Smiles can leave no patterns,
only scars fill my log.
With my deeds unwritten,
lonely stars mark my lot.

WHICH CHANGES CHANGE AGAIN

There is no earthquake or eclipse
that is as changeable as love.
The old stigmata and the crypt
now become buried and begloved.

But beware passion's turns and flips.
The embraced may reject your hugs
and hold your madness in contempt
.
And your mansion will turn to mud.
Love without reciprocity
restores your sun's calamity.

THE SOON, THE THEN, AND THE NOW

Only the poorest people
will still have live teachers
—and the richest.

Ambition wasn't to want
but to be.
Failure wasn't not to can
but to won't.
Success was not to will
but to do.

Ornatest highest steeple
adorns humble creatures.
As do bridges.

WORLDS LIVE ON BEYOND OUR WALLS AND CURTAINS

and within imaginations,
and our graspings for understanding.
I say avocados and volcanoes
are gifts from Quetzalcoatl.
And remember, we find Jesus
not only on his Hill
but also in his Garden.
And, though singular,
the Allahs reside in multitudes.
And, that Buddha planted in your field
is just one of the 28 that we know of.
And even the kami in the internet
are
infinite.

PROFESSIONS

We are not determined by our doubts.
Character is tailored by our thoughts.
We're defined by judgments and movements,
dyed and patterned by resultant actions.
A use is obedient to the hand
and purpose dependent on the mind.

Farmers embrace the sun and dirt
to encourage the wheat and the fruit.
Lumberjacks see a congress of plants
and envision a synagogue of planks.

Privateers will ascribe their profits
to themselves, perhaps to providence,
praise the powder and ball below deck,
and ignore the orphans in their wake.

This little composition, yourself,
may outlast your stiffness and bad smell.
Perhaps you'll linger for awhile
prized as a tale, epic or novel.
But even if you're a library,
audience is not eternity.

NO APOLOGY, APOLLO

Plato's septuagenarian Socrates
at his close recalled in his ladhood
learning gymnastics and poetry
but dismissed all poets as diviners
who misunderstood their message,
even as he versified his fables
and composed hymns to Apollo,
that divinity of poetry and truth,
and all the while displayed the dexterity
of his dialectic prowess in winning
the Athenian elimination round.

O, DEMOCRACY

The festival procession of spectators attends the Assembly and Sceptre debates on conditions and consequence, on revenues and revenge, while, to mend the pending amendments, the skepticals invoke their rituals to raise the specters of their freedomophile brethren and children.

WHAT MAY BE AND WHAT WILL

Child, you bear your corpse inside your mummy,
confuse eternity and brevity,
and hope for pinions.

A bivouac can become a City
if just one tent
is the dominion
of that one Prince without pause or pity
who is intent
on his ambition.

Time, geography, and identity
are all opinion.
The Prince too falls into oblivion.

THE COROLLARY

Said a walking cathedral to a tabernacle waiting,
"Human typography is the distance
between the duty and the do.
Rascality's rewarded, righteousness ruined."

To which the tabernacle replied,
"You just judge the extremes
and not the mean between."

"Just trace all their lines and angles
to see how the axiom's derived,"
said the cathedral in response.
"Everything is proved by Euclid
and by Pharaoh's red plague."

"But the spine is the body's boney Nile,"
tabernacle maintained.
"Blood is not the only medium
through which the soul perceives."

And cathedral sighed.
"So, one of us will play acute
and the other the obtuse,
no matter the pattern."

"Then," tabernacle sounded,
"let us hypotenuse together
in honor of the right."

WITNESSING

Is it preacherly
to do and say ill
and be well spoken of?
Old Testament Christians,
you enlighten yourselves
with darkness,
you hide yourselves
in nakedness,
and find fault with
my future and my fate,
my fortune and my alms.
Why haven't your mirrors
given you harm?
Character and behavior
are aspects inner and outer
of singular identity.
You post your guards
and fund their arms,
while New Testament
pagans meekly withdraw—
but in our retreat
we're not deserters
but rather warriors
seeking a firmer hold.

AND WE'VE NO ARTHUR

Mad merlins conjured
that excalibur
dubbed Tec-Knowledgey,
and any varlet
or fool can wield it
in malicious plots
'gainst our Camelot.

AN ESSAY CONCERNING HUMAN UNDERSTANDING

Innocence is the absence of experience,
while virtue is one's nature but honed and nurtured.
So is sin: it starts within, grows through practicing.
Even Locke needed both chalk and a slate to mark.

CONFESSIONS

Everyone's a politician
and everyone's a journalist,
and none of us has inhibitions.
But we all have our tales to twist.

I went to see my physician
in her office inside my tomb.
For practice, she writes out prescriptions
just to kill the kids in their wombs.

My preacher makes his confession
to the girls who are blonde and young.
He lays on his hands, as his mission,
and exhibits his gift of tongues.

Professors write dissertations
in order to hide all the facts.
And if you want real information
—oh well, you needn't even ask.

The lawyers brand themselves hired guns.
They court the richest criminals,
who transfer to them ill-gotten funds
to lie as far as laws allow.

I said I'd fill that thin co-ed
who said she hungered for new verse,
but she still starves though I'm her poet
and she's swallowed my Complete Works.

Was Jesus tacked to an easel
so Romans could paint him later?
They staged the acts of the apostles
just to build wings for their theaters.

And everyone had truth to twist
til they convinced me I was cured.
But when I asked, my psychiatrist
sneered, "Why no, I'm not even bored."

DOWSER

Once I was proudly regarded
as the foremost geographer of You:
I surveyed the careful typography
as I mapped your features anew,
measured each promontory
and charted every defile.

Many times I plumbed for your treasures
and glad continued my earthy research.
And I knew I could move
my stretched willow out
and discover sweet waters below.

But now I live in exile from You.
And now that your landscape is gone
I find – it was not your true geomancy
I'd learned. For though I'm sure
I discerned your well
I could never divine the source.

PROPERTIES

I wanted only a life unmortgaged—
how many stories I would furnish!
When I took hold of my time, my mansion,
I didn't know how still I'd be transient.

REFLECTIONS ON ERASMUS QUELLINUS II, *CUPID ON A DOLPHIN*, MUSEO DEL PRADO, MADRID

Every now is an instant
entangled with death and birth.
Most people of the present
are placeholders for the next,
random contents in life's chest.
We wonder, *What's our quest's*
destination, tide or earth?

Prophecy is an infant,
while memory is a corpse.
The future mounts his porpoise
and pursues eternal seas,
but past is pulled by horses
with the stumble and the wheeze
he occupies in his hearse.

MARILYN

Your circumference
was popular
among all the men,
but no one
sought your center,
your surface
well-traveled,
but never your atom.

Presidents, producers,
sportsmen, playwrights,
racketeers, and neighborhood boys—
your beauty
and selective promiscuity
served you well,
but at what cost
to your inner being?

DEAR READER

Sense, conception, and adequate frame—
It takes skill to write a poem
and skill too to read one.
And many works are disagreed on.
So if you can't feel my poems
there's no need for shame.

Though some poems exist to shout out loud
in all the halls and forums,
my images are blurred,
my messages and meanings obscure.
So if you can feel at home,
take a bow and feel proud!

www.ingramcontent.com/pod-product-compliance
Lightning Source LLC
Chambersburg PA
CBHW050024170726
48282CB00025B/537
* 9 7 8 8 1 1 9 2 2 8 3 8 6 *